THE
QUEEN'S
WARDROBE

To my wonderful, creative mother, Carole Golding,
who shares the late Queen's flair for colour
J.G.

First published 2021 by Two Hoots
an imprint of Pan Macmillan,
The Smithson, 6 Briset Street, London EC1M 5NR
EU representative: 1st Floor, The Liffey Trust Centre,
117-126 Sheriff Street Upper, Dublin 1, D01 YC43
Associated companies throughout the world
www.panmacmillan.com

ISBN: 978-1-5290-4552-9

7 9 8 6
A CIP catalogue record for this book is available from the British Library.
Printed in China

The illustrations in this book were created using digital media.

www.twohootsbooks.com

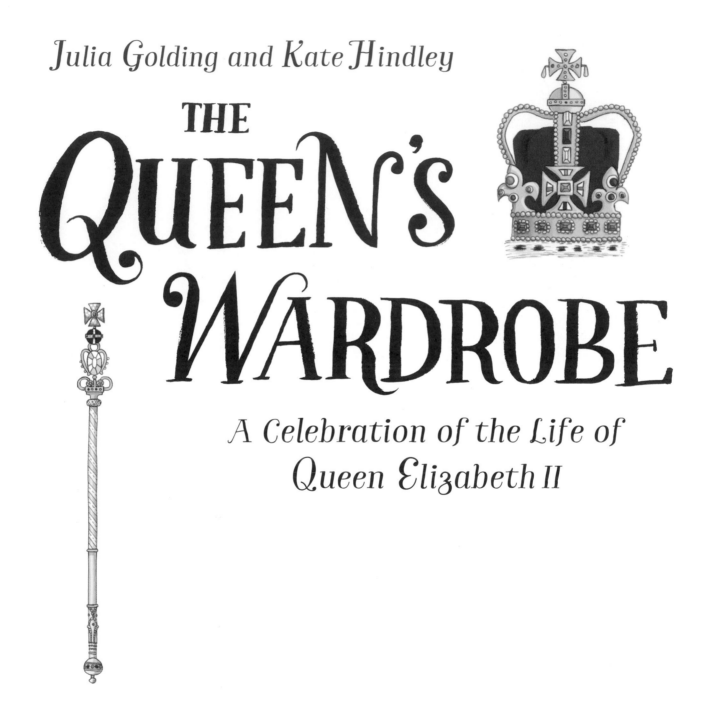

Julia Golding and Kate Hindley

THE Queen's WARDROBE

A Celebration of the Life of Queen Elizabeth II

TWO HOOTS

Contents

Foreword

*M*any of us don't spend a lot of time thinking about what we wear. We might enjoy picking a special outfit for a party, or dressing up for Halloween – or we might have to wear a uniform for school or work. But for a queen, it's very different.

Can you imagine what it would be like to get up every morning knowing that what you wear could be photographed and talked about by millions of people throughout the world?

As a costume designer for Netflix series *The Crown*, I had to recreate some of Queen Elizabeth II's most famous garments, giving me an insight into her experience as a princess and later a queen. Creating a replica of her wedding dress was a particularly daunting yet exciting experience. There are so many photographs of it and it was discussed endlessly in the press at the time, so we knew people would notice if we didn't get it right.

To begin, I read notes from the designer Norman Hartnell about the design, structure, decoration and what the dress should represent – rebirth and growth.

We then made a toile of the dress, a toile being an early version made quickly – a sort of first draft. Next we made the enormously long 4.5 metre train so the actor could practice moving and find her balance. With so many cast and crew involved, there can be no issues or accidents on the day of filming: it was vital that the dress was not only beautiful, but that it worked!

We fitted the actor maybe four or five times, making adjustments and adding details. The Queen would have gone through a similar process of rehearsal and fitting, requiring endless patience.

Because I wanted the young Queen to appear beautiful to the modern audience, I did make small adjustments to the fit of the dress, to update it slightly. I worried that the dress might look a little old-fashioned and we would lose the impact that this elegant young Queen had on the world. She was quite simply a superstar, a figurehead who represented hope for a country emerging from the horror of wartime.

To make the elaborately decorated train, we started by marking the floral design onto the fabric, then laying it out on a very long table. We employed embroiderers and students who applied beads to the stencilled pattern, carefully rolling the finished end in tissue paper as they progressed. The whole train took approximately six weeks in ten-hour shifts of six people. It was a true labour of love and the embroiderers took such pride in their achievement, much like the 350 women who made the original. I loved listening to them talk as they worked – there was a real sense of community, as there would have been back in 1947 when those dressmakers worked tirelessly for months to create a gown that would be seen across the world.

It was important to me to be extremely accurate in our recreation of the Queen's most famous outfits. This would then allow me some freedom in telling the story of the Queen's clothes in her less-documented private life.

It's my job as a costume designer to try and understand how a character feels about their clothes and how they use them to express themselves. What colours do they like and why? How do they show strength, sadness, love or vulnerability? I want to be able to show these feelings on screen using clothing, even when there is no dialogue.

The Queen always seemed happiest wearing comfortable country clothes, those associated with her childhood and outdoor pursuits. With that in mind, I used soft woollens, tartans, muted print cotton shirts and tweeds during private moments. The evening dresses I designed for Elizabeth were less stylish than her sister Margaret's, to contrast their lives and characters. For the early years of Elizabeth's marriage in Malta, I chose sun-faded cotton print dresses and skirts with soft cardigans to emphasise the carefree life of a Naval wife.

Contrast all this to the uniform-like choices of her life as a working monarch. These blocks of strong colour represent a sense of duty, the feminine equivalent of a man's suit, worn each day without too much fuss. However, the Queen did often use her jewellery, usually gifts from family, to add personal touches and messages to these working looks. She also seemed to have a love of rather witty hats. I think all this conveyed a sense of her private humour and familial affection, a hint of personality and warmth.

This carefully researched book spans nearly 100 years, with exquisite illustrations that bring to life and colour the story of one little girl growing up to become Queen, giving us a glimpse of the real woman behind the crown.

Michele Clapton

A Queen Is Born

On 21 April 1926, the Duke and Duchess of York welcomed their first child, a girl. At her christening service in Buckingham Palace on 29 May 1926, the baby was named Elizabeth Alexandra Mary Windsor. That was a lot of names for a baby, so her family called her Lilibet. Lilibet's grandfather was King George V, and her uncle, Edward, would be the next king. So there was no reason to think little Elizabeth would ever be crowned queen.

Her great-great-grandmother, Queen Victoria, had the gown made for her first child in 1841. Over the years, it was worn by another sixty-one royal babies.

There are a lot of talented people hard at work behind any gown worn by a royal – even one as small as this. The silk was woven in London, the lace came from Devon, and the gown was designed and sewn by a Scottish coalminer's daughter, Janet Sutherland. At that time, it was usually only upper-class tailors who made clothes for the royal family, so it was very unusual for Janet to be given this task.

She was later given the special title of Embroiderer to the Queen in light of her achievement. Instructions were left to wash the delicate gown only in spring water and store it in a dark room, but after many years of use, it was retired in 2004 and is now kept in a place of honour. New royal babies are christened in an exact copy, so Janet's design carries on to the new generation.

Of course, Lilibet would not remember the gown from her own christening. She noticed it though when it was worn by her younger sister, Margaret, who was born four years later in 1930.

Two Little Princesses

As Elizabeth grew up, she and her family often travelled between the city and their countryside home in Scotland, Balmoral Castle. When in London, she lived at 145 Piccadilly. The house had twenty-five bedrooms, an electric lift, a ballroom and a library. Elizabeth would carefully arrange her toy horses on the landing under the glass dome – a sign of the keen rider she would become.

There were no uniforms as Elizabeth and Margaret didn't go to school. Before the twentieth century, wealthy girls were not educated for roles outside the home, so they didn't have the choice to follow their brothers to school and university. Thanks to Victorian women who campaigned for equality, this had changed by the 1930s, but the royal family still followed the older tradition. Instead of school, the princesses had a governess, that is a teacher who lives with the family. Her name was Marion Crawford, or Crawfie. Lessons were usually finished before noon, leaving a lot of time to play, walk the corgis and ride.

The sisters were very close and this was reflected in their clothes. When Elizabeth and Margaret appeared in public, they were usually dressed in similar outfits. London meant wearing formal clothes. These might be matching coats, knee-length dresses and white hats to attend a concert, or cloaks and long silk gowns for a children's party. In the countryside, the two sisters wore clothes to play in – like sturdy knitted sweaters and tartan skirts.

In Scotland, tartan patterns show to which clan or family the wearer belongs. The royal family has several only they are entitled to wear, and one very special one called the Balmoral Tartan. The pattern was designed by Queen Victoria's husband, Prince Albert, in 1853. This tartan can only be worn by certain royal family members, and one other person: the piper at Balmoral.

KING GEORGE V

PRINCESS MARY OF TECK

WALLIS SIMPSON

KING EDWARD VIII

KING GEORGE VI

LADY ELIZABETH BOWES-LYON

PRINCESS ELIZABETH

PRINCESS MARGARET

Two New Kings

In 1936, everything changed for Elizabeth. Her grandfather, King George V, died, and his eldest son, Edward, became king. However, Edward had fallen in love with an American lady called Wallis Simpson, who had already been married. The rules were that the king couldn't marry someone who had been divorced, so after only a few months, Edward had to choose between the throne or marrying Wallis. He chose her and abdicated, meaning he would no longer be king.

Elizabeth's shy father, Albert, reluctantly became king instead of his older brother, calling himself George VI. This meant Elizabeth went from being just a minor member of the royal family to heir to the throne at only ten years old. The dress she wore to see her father crowned as King in Westminster Abbey in 1937 was specially designed for her, along with a silver and gold crown.

In that same year, when she was eleven, Elizabeth joined the Girl Guides. The Guides is a popular group for young people which encourages members to learn skills and help people. Anyone who joins promises to do their duty. Elizabeth lived by that vow all her life, doing her duty in every role she was given.

There was still time for fun. The twenty Guides and fourteen younger Brownies in the troop at Buckingham Palace went camping in the garden, cooked on campfires and learned skills like first aid. Girls from all over the country joined the Girl Guides, all wearing the same uniforms and learning the same tasks whether they were princesses or not.

The World Goes to War

In 1939, when Elizabeth was thirteen, the Second World War broke out, involving dozens of countries including Britain. It was a very frightening time for children as their fathers and brothers left to fight abroad. There was danger at home too in the form of a bombing attack called the Blitz. The Blitz damaged London and other cities, with bombs hitting houses, schools and shops as well as factories.

The King and Queen stayed in Buckingham Palace, even after a bomb hit part of the building. Children living in the most dangerous areas of the country were sent to safer places in the countryside. This was called evacuation.

The princesses spent most of the war away from London, living in Windsor Castle. Some wanted the princesses to go further away to escape the danger, as far as Canada, but their mother refused, saying the family should stay with their people.

For many years, the situation often seemed hopeless. In a time with no television or internet, people kept in touch with the news from BBC radio, and there was a special radio hour each day for children called *Children's Hour*. In the darkest days of the war, Elizabeth gave her first radio broadcast during one of these programmes to give heart to listeners across the world and reassure them that all would be well. The clothes Elizabeth wore at the time were plain,

to reflect the seriousness of the moment.

One big change during the war was the introduction of rationing, meaning limits were placed on what everyone could buy. Attacks on cargo ships led to a scarcity of many goods, including fabric. Elizabeth's outfits began to be made from cloth purchased with ration coupons. Dresses used less material and fashions became plainer so nothing was wasted.

A rare chance to dress up came when Elizabeth and Margaret staged pantomimes with friends to raise money for the war effort. Using the splendid props and clothes they found in the attics of Windsor Castle, Elizabeth played the prince in *Cinderella*, with Margaret in the title role.

Elizabeth the Mechanic

During the war, Elizabeth became an adult. In 1943, she made her first official visit, which meant she represented the royal family at a public event. It was a visit to the Grenadier Guards, the army regiment in which she was a colonel. As she neared eighteen, the law was changed so she could rule in her father's place when he was abroad or ill. Before then, a young royal had to be over twenty-one to qualify so Elizabeth was the first prince or princess to be given this role.

Like other young people of her age, Elizabeth had war work to do. In 1945, she joined the Auxiliary Territorial Service (ATS), the women's branch of the army. Along with other women taking on ground-breaking roles, Elizabeth trained as a driver and a mechanic. In addition to her smart khaki uniform, she also wore overalls for the messy jobs. War on such a large scale brought changes to the way women were seen. Though women were not allowed to fight, many served in army support units, or took over jobs traditionally done by men, becoming military police officers, messengers and radar operators. Women proved they were up to any job. A future queen who knew her way around a lorry engine fitted right in!

★ ★ ★ One Penny

VICTORY!

Winston Churchill and members of the Royal Family join celebrating crowds from the balcony of Buckingham Palace.

On 8 May 1945, victory in Europe was declared. Elizabeth and Margaret joined their parents and Prime Minister Winston Churchill on the balcony of Buckingham Palace to greet the crowds celebrating the peace. Seeing the huge party in the street below, Elizabeth asked the King and Queen if she and Margaret could go and join in – in secret. This was really exciting for the princesses as they were not usually allowed to mix with ordinary people, but that day the rulebook was torn up! Hidden among the strangers linking arms, the princesses were swept along on what Elizabeth described as 'the tide of happiness and relief'.

Ration-Book Wedding Dress

There was a secret side to Elizabeth's life during the war: she was falling in love. She first crossed paths with her future husband, Prince Philip of Greece and Denmark, at a wedding in 1934. They met again in 1939 at Britannia Royal Naval College in Dartmouth and the sporty young cadet made a great impression on her by jumping over the tennis nets! The sweethearts wrote to each other during the war, as Philip was serving in the navy. When the war ended, and their thoughts turned to marriage, they struggled to convince their families that they made a good match. But the couple did not give up, and eventually won Elizabeth's father's permission – which was an important part of a royal marriage proposal.

The public knew very little about this, because Elizabeth's father had asked the couple to keep their relationship secret until she turned twenty-one. The next year, the engagement was announced and they were married. It was a new kind of royal wedding for a new era because, unlike Queen Victoria, the future queen decided to keep her own name rather than take her husband's surname, Mountbatten.

The wedding was held on 20 November 1947 at Westminster Abbey. Britain was still recovering from the war, so it was an uplifting moment that everyone could enjoy. Rationing was still in place, and even a royal like Elizabeth had to buy the material for her dress with coupons. The designer was Norman Hartnell, who would be the Queen's favourite dressmaker for many years to come. To make the right splash, the government donated an extra 200 coupons. Rationing coupons were not allowed to be swapped, but many brides around the country offered their spares – which Elizabeth returned. A princess couldn't break the rules.

The gown had long sleeves and was made from Chinese silk, decorated with crystals and pearls. The flowers and wheat ears on the dress symbolized rebirth and hope.

1948

1949

1950

1951

Taking the Throne

In 1948 a son, Charles, was born to Elizabeth and Philip, followed two years later by a daughter, Anne. Elizabeth divided her time between official duties, her children and spending time with her husband, whose naval job took him to Malta, in the Mediterranean. She loved the sunny island but, sadly, her father's health was getting worse. As the King was unable to go abroad for official visits, Elizabeth and Philip went in his place, travelling in 1952 to Kenya, the first stop on a world tour. One day, the news came that Elizabeth's father had died and she was now Queen. It was a terrible shock – and meant they had to hurry home immediately.

Elizabeth began her royal duties at once, but it was decided to wait a year for the coronation. Her favourite designer, Norman Hartnell, set about the task of creating her coronation gown, this time working in white satin. The embroidery alone took the workers 3,500 hours over three months! The dress was decorated with the emblems of England, Scotland, Wales and Northern Ireland, as well as the Commonwealth (a larger group of countries of which the Queen was head). Can you spot any you recognize? Olive branches and wheat ears were included as symbols of peace and plenty.

Over the gown, Elizabeth wore the traditional purple coronation robe. Made by Ede & Ravenscroft, robemakers to the royal household since 1689, it was five and a half metres long and trimmed with fur. The heaviness of the gown and robe would have reminded the Queen of the seriousness of her new duties, not to mention the weight of the crown itself!

E II R

1952

The Crown Jewels

The royal family has a very special collection of jewels and precious objects, which together are called the Crown Jewels. The most historic are kept in the Tower of London under guard. The centrepiece is St Edward's Crown, which the Queen wore for her coronation. Created for Charles II in 1661, it was named after St Edward the Confessor, one of the first kings of England. Made from solid gold and covered in jewels, it weighs over 2 kg – that's like balancing two bags of potatoes on your head!

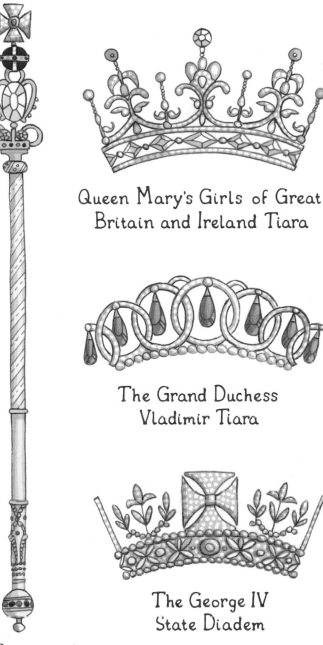

Queen Mary's Girls of Great Britain and Ireland Tiara

The Grand Duchess Vladimir Tiara

The George IV State Diadem

Protector of Good

St Edward's Crown

The Sovereign's Sceptre

The Imperial State Crown

St Edward's Crown is only worn for coronations, and it is the Imperial State Crown that is seen most often. It is set with nearly 3,000 jewels, including the Cullinan II diamond, cut from the biggest gem-quality diamond ever found, and the Black Prince's Ruby, which is the big red gem at the front. The Imperial crown weighs just over 1 kg so you can understand why, when she reached the age of ninety-three, the Queen decided to stop wearing it.

Queen Victoria's Crown
Ruby Brooch

The Flower Basket Brooch

Despite having so many wonderful jewels to choose from, the Queen was most often seen in a simple three-strand pearl necklace, a gift from her parents.

The Cullinan V Brooch

The Grima Ruby Brooch

The Queen Anne
and
Queen Caroline
Pearl Necklaces

The Burmese Rubies

The Brazilian Aquamarine
Parure

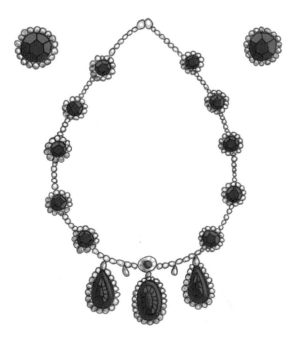

The Queen Mary Fringe Tiara

ATLANTIC OCEAN

COMMONWEALTH TOUR

LONDON CANADA AUSTRALIA INDIA

NEW ZEALAND

OPENING CANADIAN PARLIAMENT 1957

NORTH AMERICA

NORTH ATLANTIC OCEAN

EUROPE

AFRICA

LAUNCHING THE ROYAL YACHT BRITANNIA 1953

SOUTH AMERICA

LONDON 2000

Commonwealth Colours

For hundreds of years, Britain conquered other countries to add to its empire. At the start of the twentieth century, Britain ruled nations all over the world from afar, but opposition to this system was growing. Gradually these colonized nations broke away in order to govern themselves, and the empire came to an end. Many of these countries joined a group of friendly independent nations called the Commonwealth. At the beginning of the Queen's reign, there were only eight members; now there are fifty-four! The British monarch is head of this organization, and remains Head of State in some of these countries.

The Queen's schedule always gave over part of the year to visiting Commonwealth countries. She spent November 1953 to May 1954 on the longest of those trips (70,000 km).

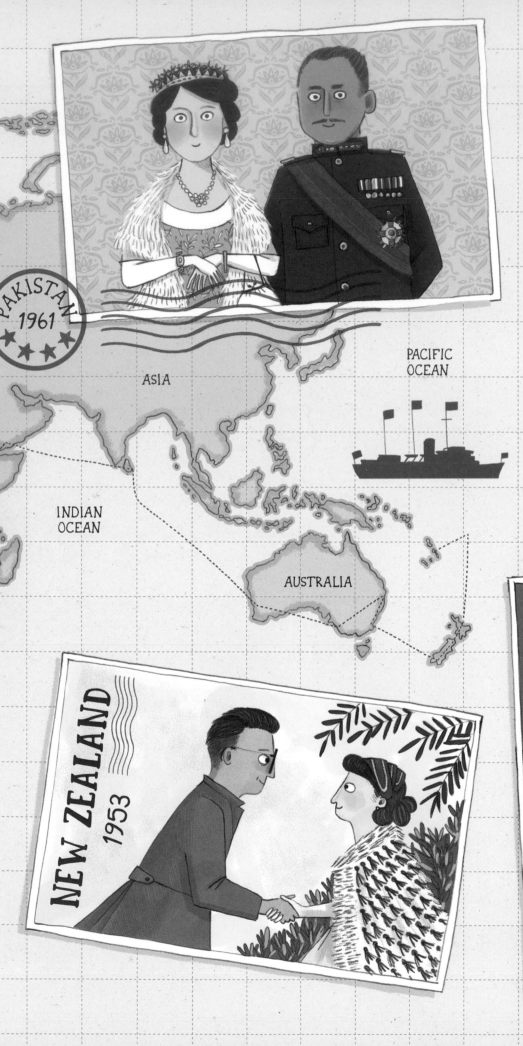

Many outfits were needed to suit all the places the royal tour visited, from sundresses to warm coats. While the Queen was most often seen in single colours, she sometimes wore patterns or combinations of colours that reflected the nation she was visiting. At a dinner in Lahore in 1961, she wore an evening dress in the national colours of Pakistan: green and white. In 1974, on tour in Australia, she wore a yellow dress embroidered with the national flower, the wattle.

Sometimes the Queen's hosts would give her gifts to wear. Nelson Mandela, then President of South Africa, gave her a scarf with a pattern depicting bushmen from his home in the Eastern Cape hunting antelope. Perhaps the most striking gift of all was the traditional Maori feather cloak, a chief's symbol, that was given to her in New Zealand on the 1953 tour (Prince Philip got one too).

The Swinging 60s

Ten years into Elizabeth's reign, a decade of rapid change began for Britain. The economy began to do well, British culture was finding a new audience worldwide and British fashion was setting trends.

Yet at the beginning of the 1960s, the Queen and the country appeared very behind the times. When President Kennedy and his glamorous wife, Jackie, visited the Queen, the contrast between the first ladies was clear. Only three years younger than Elizabeth, Jackie wore a stylish, modern gown, while the Queen chose an A-line dress by her old favourite, Norman Hartnell. His designs made her look mature and stable, but not as exciting as America's First Lady.

Then came a burst of creativity from across Britain. The thrilling new Liverpool-based band, The Beatles, shot to fame. Their music went through many styles during the 1960s, from rock and roll to the experimental music of the hippy movement. In 1965, the Queen gave the Beatles an award called the MBE, much to the annoyance of more traditional people who didn't think such honours should go to pop stars. British fashion was at the cutting edge, too. Mary Quant became famous for introducing the mini dress, as well as hot pants (very short shorts).

How did Queen Elizabeth respond as head of a newly fashionable country? Her clothes became slightly more modern, flavoured by the new style but not going all out, except for the occasional flourish of a daring hat! Maybe she decided that radical new fashions were best left to the younger generation?

The Spectacular 70s

I n the 1970s, Britain underwent yet more deep changes, but of a more serious kind. Economic trouble hit, and the whole world experienced a difficult time as there was a global shortage of oil, to make fuel. But while the country struggled, flamboyant fashion thrived, with tie-dyes, huge flares, high platform shoes and frilly shirts becoming popular.

How did the Queen's wardrobe reflect these times? She certainly didn't follow the trends of white disco suits, flashy glam rock or punk clothes held together with safety pins! Instead she took a direction that became her signature, or typical, look, choosing bold single colour outfits, called 'colour blocking'. This was so that people could see her easily. At only 160 cm tall (5'3") she knew she might otherwise fade into the crowds. This is why she often chose bright colours like lemon, lime, hot pink, orange or red.

The 1970s was the decade when most people first got a colour television, so maybe this also influenced the Queen's choice. She celebrated twenty-five years on the throne in 1977, with her Silver Jubilee celebrations broadcast in colour to hundreds of millions of viewers across the world.

The designer Hardy Amies, who had been making clothes for the Queen since the 1950s, brought some more daring looks into the Queen's wardrobe around this time. He created her two most famous Silver Jubilee outfits: a pink day dress and matching hat with dangling blossoms, and the white beaded gown that appeared on nearly all the souvenirs from that year.

Few Trousers, Lots of Hats

It was rare to see the Queen in trousers. In her youth, it was because girls traditionally dressed in skirts or dresses and the boys in shorts – no trousers for either. But over the twentieth century, fashions changed, partly due to women's war work requiring practical clothing and partly due to a shift in attitudes. It became normal for women and girls to wear trousers.

There were a handful of times when the Queen wore trousers in public. She wore a black pair on a state visit to New Zealand. She was also seen wearing a smart grey trouser suit in 2003 when leaving hospital after a knee operation, possibly to hide the bandage. Other times have also been for practical reasons – on safari or when travelling. Yet there's one time when the Queen always wore trousers: while riding! She loved jodhpurs (riding trousers) and even into her nineties still wore them to ride.

Aldershot,
UK
1938

London,
UK
1949

Australia
1954

Nigeria
1956

India
1961

Canterbury,
UK
1965

Germany
1965

Ottawa,
Canada
1967

Coventry,
UK
1970

Mexico
1975

Kuwait
1979

Tuvalu
1982

Solomon Islands
1982

Shanghai,
China
1986

Barbados
1989

The Queen was born at a time when it was almost unthinkable to go out without a hat, for both men and women. The Queen had very specific requirements for her hats. They had to match her outfit and have shallow brims so her face could be seen. Hats were also an opportunity for some more daring fashion choices, such as the bright yellow number designed by Simone Mirman that the Queen wore on a visit to Germany in 1965 – nicknamed the 'yellow spaghetti hat'.

Washington,
USA
1991

Ascot,
UK
2004

London Zoo,
UK
2016

Singapore
2006

Hillsborough Castle,
UK
2014

Dressing Up

As one of a long line of monarchs reaching back for centuries, the Queen inherited many unusual ceremonies. After the Coronation, her most glittering outfit could be seen at the State Opening of Parliament where she usually dressed in a white gown and red velvet train, along with some of the Crown Jewels.

Another colourful royal ceremony is the Order of the Garter. It was created in medieval times by Edward III, inspired by the stories of King Arthur and the Round Table. In addition to the senior royals, there are twenty-four knights and ladies. Members of the Order wear a special velvet robe, plumed hat and red sash at the annual procession on Garter Day.

Maundy Thursday before Easter brings a ceremony where the monarch gives out purses of money (one red, one white) to recognize elderly people for helping their community.

Perhaps the most spectacular ceremony of all is Trooping the Colour. Over 1,400 soldiers, 200 horses and 400 musicians march for the monarch. The Queen used to ride in this ceremony herself, wearing a Guards Regiment uniform and long skirt for riding side-saddle. In 1981, the ceremony took a dramatic turn when a man fired six blank shots at her from the crowd in the Mall. The Queen managed to control her horse, Burmese, while the police arrested the attacker. She carried on riding a horse to the ceremony up until 1987, when she switched to arriving in a carriage.

Dressing Down

After her children married, the Queen soon became a grandmother. Her first grandchild was born in 1977 to her daughter, Anne. After her son Charles married Lady Diana Spencer, two new princes arrived: William and Harry. In 2015, she signed into law a change making girls equal to boys in the line to inherit the throne.

When at home with family, the Queen liked to wear comfortable, practical clothes. She favoured fabrics such as tweed, tartan and knitwear, matched with stout shoes or wellies. These suited her favourite outdoor pursuits, which included gardening and walking her dogs.

The Queen kept her clothes for as long as possible. When, in 2012, the coat manufacturer Barbour offered her a new jacket for her Diamond Jubilee, she opted to have her old one spruced up instead.

One famous 'dress down' look for the Queen was her headscarf. Sometimes the scarf signalled a sad moment. One of her lowest points came in 1992 when part of Windsor Castle was destroyed in a fire and, two weeks later, Charles and Diana separated. The Queen made a rare public statement that it had been her *Annus horribilis*, Latin for 'horrible year'. Seeing her walking around the burnt-out building in her headscarf fitted this mood. By contrast, the headscarf was also worn at moments of freedom and happiness. In her downtime, she often raced around in her Range Rover, headscarf in place.

Speaking To the People

One of the duties of the monarch is speaking to the country. The Queen gave her first address when she was only fourteen during the Second World War.

The public could see what the Queen wore for her speeches from the first televised Christmas message in 1957. George V, the Queen's grandfather, began the tradition of addressing the nation at Christmas in 1932 and it continues to this day. In the first years, when television was only in black and white, the Queen chose fabrics that would sparkle. She wore short sleeves and no coat to show that she was at home, like her viewers. In the first colour broadcast in 1967, she chose a lemon-yellow dress to celebrate the arrival of colour with a pop!

Apart from her annual Christmas broadcast, the Queen only spoke directly to the nation on six other televised occasions. Two of these were when members of the royal family died – Princess Diana in 1997 and the Queen Mother in 2002. As people often do for a funeral, she dressed all in black. In 2020, the Queen made a rare TV appearance during the coronavirus lockdown to give thanks and rally the nation. She wore a simple green dress with her usual three-string necklace of pearls.

The most epic of all her appearances was at the opening ceremony of the London Summer Olympics in 2012, directed by film-maker Danny Boyle. The Queen took part in a video that saw her escorted to a helicopter by film spy James Bond (played by Daniel Craig) and flown to the Olympic Stadium. At the ceremony itself, the audience of thousands let out a gasp as the Queen appeared to leap out of the helicopter hovering above (although in reality it may have been a stuntman in a wig, wearing a copy of the Queen's sugar-pink beaded dress).

Our Record-Breaking Queen

On 9 September 2016, Queen Elizabeth II officially became Britain's longest-reigning monarch, beating the record of sixty-three years and seven months set by her great-great-grandmother, Queen Victoria. When she died on 8 September 2022, the Queen was the world's longest-serving female monarch.

Every few years after a monarch takes the throne, anniversary celebrations take place called Jubilees – each represented by a precious metal or stone. The Queen celebrated a Silver (twenty-five years), Golden (fifty), Diamond (sixty), Sapphire (sixty-five) and Platinum Jubilee (seventy). The Diamond Jubilee celebrations involved a parade of 670 boats, including the 27-metre barge Gloriana. For the Platinum Jubilee there was a hot air balloon regatta and street parties across the country.

The Queen held the record for the monarch with the most coins bearing her portrait, appearing on money in at least thirty-five countries. She was the world's most widely travelled monarch, having covered well over a million miles by plane, boat and train.

The Queen met thousands of heads of state, including thirteen US presidents, and saw fifteen British prime ministers take office (including Winston Churchill, the famous wartime leader). She could fairly claim to have shaken hands with more people over her long life than anyone else. These included inspirational leaders from Nelson Mandela of South Africa to girl's education campaigner, Malala Yousafzai. She owned over thirty corgis but there is no mention of any cats. For every one of these impressive records, Queen Elizabeth II always had the perfect wardrobe, wearing a rainbow of colours — from beautiful gowns, to practical uniforms, to comfortable raincoats and wellies.

Note from the Author

I had great fun sifting through endless articles and online museum archives while researching this book, as well as the brilliant *Young Elizabeth* by Kate Williams and *Our Rainbow Queen* by Sali Hughes. The Royal Collection, Historic Royal Palaces and Victoria and Albert Museum websites are all good places to find out more about the royal wardrobe (with parental help).

I would like to acknowledge the work of the many exceptional designers who are responsible for the outfits and jewels worn by Queen Elizabeth II throughout her long reign. Designers whose outfits are featured in this book include Norman Hartnell, Ian Thomas, Hardy Amies, Stewart Parvin, Burberry and Hermès (scarves), Anello & Davide (shoes), Launer (handbags), Frederick Fox, Rachel Trevor-Morgan and Simone Mirman (hats).

I would like to pay tribute, too, to the many seamstresses and other garment workers who had a part in creating the clothes that filled the Queen's wardrobe. And, of course, Angela Kelly, the Queen's Personal Advisor and Senior Dresser, and her favourite designer.

The Queen's reign came to an end when she died peacefully at Balmoral Castle on the 8 September 2022 at the age of 96. How apt for a queen who wore rainbow colours that a real rainbow appeared over Windsor Castle as the announcement of her passing was made. I hope this book is a fitting celebration of her life and achievements.

Julia Golding